THE REAL ESTATE RENEGADE

"HOW SAM ZELL BUILT A BILLION-DOLLAR EMPIRE"

BASH OT. BETH

TABLE OF CONTENTS

CHAPTER 1 6

THE EARLY DAYS OF A MAVERICK 6

1.1 Growing Up in Chicago: Family, Values, and Influence 6

1.2 Discovering Real Estate: Sam Zell's First Deals and Lessons 12

CHAPTER 2 23

THE ART OF THE DEAL 23

2.1 A Different Perspective: Zell's Unique Approach to Negotiation 23

2.2 The Big Break: Pivotal Acquisitions That Launched an Empire 29

CHAPTER 3 39

CALCULATED RISK AND REWARD 39

3.1 Embracing Uncertainty: Zell's Bold Moves in High-Stakes Markets 39

3.2 Timing the Market: How Zell Mastered the Cycles of Real Estate .. 47

CHAPTER 4 56

BUILDING AN EMPIRE 56

4.1 From Office Spaces to Trailer Parks: Diversifying the Portfolio 56

4.2 The Importance of Personnel: Building a Successful Team 64

CHAPTER 5 74

BREAKING CONVENTIONS 74

5.1 The Contrarian Mindset: Zell's Approach to Conventional Wisdom. 74

5.2 Converting Problems into Possibilities: Managing Economic Declines 82

CHAPTER 6 92

THE ZELL WAY: PRINCIPLES FOR SUCCESS 92

6.1 Resilience and Grit: Overcoming Setbacks in Business and Life 92

6.2 The Long Game: Zell's Enduring Philosophy on Wealth and Legacy. 100

CHAPTER 7 110

THE REAL ESTATE RENEGADE'S LEGACY 110

7.1 Philanthropy and Impact: Zell's Influence Beyond Real Estate 110

7.2 Zell's Blueprint for Future Entrepreneurs: Lessons for the Next Generation 119

CHAPTER 1

THE EARLY DAYS OF A MAVERICK

1.1 Growing Up in Chicago: Family, Values, and Influence

The start of Sam Zell's journey takes place in Chicago, a city that would serve as a foundation and a starting point for his unique path.

Zell was born on September 28, 1941, to Jewish immigrants who had fled the atrocities of World War II Poland, inheriting a legacy of resilience, survival, and ingenuity from his family.

After escaping the Nazi invasion of Poland, Ruchla and Berek Zielonka, later known as Rochelle and Bernard Zell, made Chicago their home. Bernard was a diligent and innovative wholesaler of jewelry, while Rochelle was recognized for her sharp intelligence and straightforward demeanor.

Unitedly, they instilled in their home the principles that influenced Zell's entrepreneurial way of thinking: a respect for diligence, a dedication to loved ones, and a readiness to take on challenges.

Zell grew up on the North Side of Chicago and lived the life of a family of first-generation immigrants. His parents emphasized the importance of education and ingrained a solid work ethic in him. Bernard, a self-taught individual who speaks multiple languages and has strong business skills, educated Zell on the significance of being resourceful.

Even with his busy work schedule, his father managed to find time for meaningful discussions about the importance of money, the power of resilience, and the value of independence.

On the contrary, Rochelle motivated Zell to explore his intellectual curiosity, prompting him to think critically and form his viewpoints instead of adhering to tradition.

These experiences nurtured a mindset Zell would later describe as "contrarian" — a readiness to challenge conventions and welcome potentially risky concepts.

As a young child, Zell showed early signs of his entrepreneurial mindset. Once he turned 12 years old, he started making money by purchasing and selling Playboy magazines and delivering newspapers as a paperboy.

Zell's entrepreneurial projects were not just pastimes; they served as his learning experience. He perfected his abilities in recognizing market demands, comprehending customer inclinations, and generating value.

The diverse range of cultures, businesses, and urban obstacles in Chicago provided an ideal environment for young Zell to nurture these characteristics. The fast pace and energy of the city would later motivate Zell's vision for a real estate empire that represented both determination and flexibility.

During his time in high school, Zell consistently pushed himself by participating in debates often and reading a lot.

He had a strong interest in economics and history, recognizing that they were crucial for achieving success.

Zell's list of books to read consisted of biographies of courageous individuals from history, specifically focusing on those who had taken risks or paved the way in business or politics.

Reading these stories gave him insight into the lives of individuals who had transformed their environments, and Zell started envisioning his future in a similar light. The impact of his parents' immigrant heritage is significant and should not be underestimated.

Coming to America with limited resources, his parents emphasized the significance of financial security and autonomy while also acknowledging the value of taking calculated risks — a principle that deeply resonated with Zell.

His parents' sacrifices made him determined to succeed and aware of the unpredictable nature of circumstances.

This mindset became the basis for his future attitude towards risk: Zell was never careless, but he was bold in identifying opportunities that went unnoticed by others. Risk for Zell transformed into a tool to handle with caution, instead of something to steer clear of.

This approach would eventually shape his strategy in the real estate sector, as he became adept at recognizing opportunities in situations perceived as risky by others.

1.2 Discovering Real Estate: Sam Zell's First Deals and Lessons

Zell's curiosity in the real estate industry was ignited unexpectedly while he was attending the University of Michigan. During his time as a college student, he first considered a career in law or business. Nevertheless, destiny took a different course when a fraternity brother introduced him to the realm of student housing.

Zell promptly identified that there was an overlooked market for student housing. College students were a consistent, recurring demographic that had a strong need for affordable and well-kept housing.

Zell's intuition guided him to make a daring choice: to personally venture into the student housing industry.

Zell's initial business endeavor had substantial outcomes despite its modest size. He successfully persuaded landlords to allow him to rent their properties at reduced prices, assuring them that he would take care of upkeep and finding tenants. Zell understood that his competitive edge came from his skill in comprehending his target audience, who were college students.

Ensuring a steady need for his properties near the university, he decided to offer inexpensive and well-kept housing options.

Furthermore, being on campus enabled him to serve as a mediator between tenants and landlords, guaranteeing that concerns were dealt with quickly.

Zell quickly gained a reliable reputation by directly engaging with customers and truly understanding their needs.

From these initial transactions, Zell gained two crucial insights: Firstly, he grasped the significance of knowing his customers and identifying the distinct requirements of various market sectors.

Student housing, specifically, needed a unique management strategy, since residents were frequently younger and had less experience with tasks such as paying rent and caring for the property.

Zell customized his services to address these difficulties by introducing effective rent collection procedures and prompt maintenance services that met the demands of his tenants.

Zell's second lesson was that successful business ventures can be replicated if they have a strong foundation, known as scaling up.

After witnessing the success of his first units, Zell scaled up his business by buying additional properties and collaborating with more property owners.

When Zell graduated, he had developed a small yet successful collection of real estate. It was more than just the cash; he was perfecting a business plan that could be used for any future real estate projects.

Zell's triumph in student housing affirmed his conviction in seeking out unorthodox prospects, particularly those with great potential and minimal competition.

While attending law school at the University of Michigan, Zell kept investing in real estate and noticed he was paying more attention to wider market trends.

During this time, he shifted from being directly involved in managing properties to developing his skills as a strategist.

He came to understand that real estate involved more than just structures and property; it was about utilizing assets, comprehending cycles, and making well-timed investments.

Zell researched economic indicators, monitored updates on urban development, and participated in city planning meetings. Zell's dedication to comprehending the wider scope of his investments made him unique and built his reputation as someone who not only noticed overlooked opportunities but also acted on them.

Upon finishing his education, Zell came back to Chicago and officially started working in the real estate sector.

However, unlike a lot of his colleagues, Zell was not drawn to "secure" investments. Instead of that, he sought out distressed properties and assets in markets that were undervalued.

Zell understood that even though many investors preferred well-known, popular areas, he could uncover potential in ignored locations or abandoned properties. Zell's skill in recognizing these underpriced assets became his distinguishing characteristic. His approach focused not only on buying real estate but on adding value in overlooked areas.

Zell's initial transactions in Chicago were very profitable, where he could purchase at a low price, improve the value of the property, and make a profit through selling or renting.

One of Zell's initial significant purchases was a multi-unit property located in a less appealing area of Chicago.

His plan involved refurbishing the units, enhancing safety and aesthetics, and targeting middle-income families and young professionals in the marketing process. By doing that, he converted a neglected structure into a desirable place to live. Even though it was an unorthodox method, it was exactly the type of project that Zell enjoyed.

This property not only yielded a significant ROI but also validated Zell's belief that there is frequently unrecognized potential in "undesirable" locations.

By going through these experiences, Zell developed a structure that would shape his future transactions: search for worth in overlooked areas, stay connected to market needs, and boldly challenge conventional thinking.

When he founded Equity Group Investments, his first real estate company, he had already created a successful formula that went against traditional beliefs.

Conclusion

Sam Zell's early life embodies a mix of perseverance, inquisitiveness, and readiness to embrace challenges, traits that would define his professional journey.

His upbringing in Chicago, his roots in immigration, and his introduction to student housing all set the foundation for the empire he would eventually create.

Zell's path is characterized by persistent determination and sharp understanding of both individuals and markets, leading him to become not just a billionaire but also a renowned figure in the real estate industry.

CHAPTER 2

THE ART OF THE DEAL

2.1 A Different Perspective: Zell's Unique Approach to Negotiation

Sam Zell's unique negotiation technique was not traditional and frequently opposing, showcasing his capacity to look past the evidence and capitalize on possibilities that others neglected.

In contrast to his colleagues who viewed deals as win-lose situations, Zell took a more comprehensive approach, recognizing that deals were most enduring when all involved parties gained value.

To Zell, a prosperous negotiation was more than just achieving victory or getting the most favorable terms; it involved building connections, recognizing distinct value propositions, and most importantly, comprehending the motivations of all parties.

Zell's main principle was to place importance on comprehension rather than aggression. Zell thought that an effective negotiator was a person who actively listened and posed thoughtful questions.

He frequently recommended his team not to make quick judgments, but to focus on understanding the true desires of the other party.

Zell saw each deal as a mystery to solve, with the solution lying in understanding the other side's interests and limitations.

Zell once stated that understanding another person's viewpoint is the key aspect of negotiation.

This method provided him with a competitive advantage. Instead of adhering to conventional metrics or expectations, Zell had a talent for recognizing unappreciated value in deals.

An example would be Zell's ability to recognize the potential of distressed assets or envision enhancements that could greatly increase the property's market value during property acquisition negotiations.

His experience with purchasing and remodeling student housing in college showed him that the value of the property was not just in its physical assets, but also in the operational enhancements and customer service improvements made after acquiring it.

Zell's approach to negotiation also included a strong acceptance of uncertainty and danger.

Although some investors avoided transactions without defined terms or possible risks, Zell was ready to enter into deals that others were hesitant about.

Viewing ambiguity as a chance was seen by him– an area where fewer rivals were brave enough to explore.

Zell was recognized for his skill in staying composed when faced with pressure, seldom fazed by unexpected alterations or obstacles. He saw such circumstances as a normal part of the journey, enabling him to negotiate better terms while others were scared off by the unknown.

Zell's initial strategy included what he referred to as "knowing the right time to leave." He followed a rule: he would walk away without hesitation if a deal didn't meet his value criteria or compromised his principles.

The readiness to walk away from discussions commanded a level of admiration from colleagues. It was clear to everyone that Zell was determined and willing to be patient for a more favorable deal.

Leaving was not a mere trick; it was a sincere belief that helped him stay on track with negotiations that matched his goals.

Aside from his keen observations and fearless approach, Zell possessed a clever sense of humor that proved advantageous during negotiations.

Recognized for his straightforwardness and wit, he was able to ease tension with a joke or cut through formalities with a frank observation.

This frequently caught people off guard, which put him in a favorable position as they became less defensive and more ready to communicate openly.

Zell's natural personality, not just a strategy, was suited to this approach, creating a calm yet focused ambiance during negotiations.

2.2 The Big Break: Pivotal Acquisitions That Launched an Empire

Although Zell was known for his distinctive negotiation style, it was his strategic purchases that distinguished him in the competitive real estate industry.

He got his first big opportunity by purchasing troubled commercial properties in the tough economic times of the 1970s.

During this time of elevated inflation and economic unpredictability, numerous property owners were finding it difficult to cope with increasing expenses, and Zell identified an opportunity to purchase valuable real estate at a reduced price.

His gut feeling indicated that the market would bounce back, and when it did, the properties he purchased would increase significantly in value.

One of the most significant investments he made during this period was buying a commercial property in the heart of Chicago's downtown area.

Several investors viewed the property as a hopeless case because of the area's economic downturn, but Zell saw a chance to make a positive change.

Zell was able to raise the value of the property greatly in just a few years by renovating, updating infrastructure, and securing trustworthy tenants through leasing. This agreement showcased his ability to recognize worth in situations others viewed as risky, serving as a model for his upcoming purchases.

The establishment of Equity Group Investments (EGI) in the early 1970s was the next significant achievement.

Zell aimed to establish a company with EGI that could manage acquisitions on a large scale, enabling him to take advantage of opportunities in various markets.

EGI, under Zell's guidance, gained a reputation for its capacity to handle troubled assets and create value from difficult circumstances. Zell utilized the platform to obtain assets that were not performing well in various sectors such as office buildings, shopping centers, and multi-family housing units.

Zell quickly became a prominent figure in real estate thanks to EGI's varied collection of properties.

Zell's crucial moment occurred in the mid-1980s when he spearheaded one of the earliest real estate investment trusts (REITs).

The deal permitted him to combine multiple properties into one publicly traded company, allowing investors to invest in real estate without owning property themselves.

At that time, this action was groundbreaking by providing liquidity to an asset class that was typically illiquid, enabling Zell to access fresh capital.

Zell's REIT allowed institutional investors to participate in real estate and was so successful that it was soon widely adopted in the industry.

The REIT structure he created not only attracted fresh funds into real estate but also boosted Zell's standing and impact across the nation.

Another important purchase happened when Zell chose to venture into the manufactured housing industry.

Numerous real estate investors overlooked mobile home parks, considering them to be properties of low value with limited growth potential.

However, Zell recognized the opportunity in this undervalued asset class. Zell recognized that managing manufactured housing efficiently could result in a stable tenant base and low turnover, which would lead to strong, consistent cash flow.

Zell's manufactured housing portfolio eventually became a highly successful segment of his empire, demonstrating his talent for transforming neglected assets into lucrative investments.

As Zell expanded his empire, his capacity to pursue bigger, more intricate purchases also increased. During the early 1990s, he targeted office buildings and retail properties in top locations throughout the United States. His focus was on properties in cities with strong potential for growth, like Los Angeles, New York, and Miami.

During this time, one of his most triumphant purchases was acquiring a portfolio of office buildings in downtown Los Angeles.

Zell understood that despite the current decrease in the area's economic activity, the city's solid economic foundation indicated promising future growth opportunities.

He was prepared to retain ownership of the properties until the market improved, and this decision proved to be successful when property values in the area increased significantly. Zell believed in being opportunistic by being bold when others were scared, allowing him to benefit from undervalued assets in times of economic hardship.

One of his most notable purchases occurred in the early 2000s when he ventured into the newspaper industry, a decision that was considered risky by many due to the declining profits in the industry.

Zell purchased the Tribune Company, which included the Chicago Tribune and Los Angeles Times, along with other publications.

While the acquisition didn't bring the financial success Zell expected, it highlighted his openness to exploring new areas and taking risks that others shied away from. For Zell, the Tribune acquisition was as focused on the challenge as it was on making money.

Zell showcased a distinctive mix of patience, strategic foresight, and timing in all of these acquisitions.

He had no fear of investing in markets that others had given up on and was not worried about keeping properties for long periods if he thought they would increase in value over time.

Zell was aware that real estate cycles were unavoidable, and by matching his purchases with long-term patterns, he continuously transformed possible threats into profitable returns.

Conclusion

Sam Zell's success in the real estate industry was largely due to his skill in securing innovative deals.

His ability to negotiate and think differently enabled him to obtain troubled assets and generate value that others overlooked.

Zell's negotiating style combined strategy, flexibility, and humor, and his investments, ranging from troubled office buildings to the establishment of REITs, demonstrated his vision and courage.

CHAPTER 3

CALCULATED RISK AND REWARD

3.1 Embracing Uncertainty: Zell's Bold Moves in High-Stakes Markets

Sam Zell is frequently labeled as a "contrarian investor," someone who not only accepts uncertainty but actively looks for opportunities in situations perceived as risky by others.

Zell found high-stakes markets to be a profitable environment due to the fact that they were intimidating to others.

To him, turbulent markets or economic recessions were a chance to discover unseen possibilities and take advantage of assets that had been devalued because of temporary instability. One of Zell's fundamental beliefs was recognizing the inherent connection between risk and reward.

Instead of steering clear of high-risk markets, Zell created a method to assess the potential of these markets.

This was particularly noticeable in the 1970s and 1980s as the economy went through phases of high inflation, causing significant uncertainty throughout industries, particularly in real estate.

The market was full of undervalued properties as owners rushed to sell assets they could no longer afford. Nonetheless, Zell viewed this as a chance to buy troubled properties at a large discount, believing that the economy would eventually recover and these investments would become valuable again.

Zell's foray into prefabricated housing demonstrates his willingness to take risks in non-traditional industries.

When he started buying manufactured housing, the real estate industry did not recognize the worth of mobile home parks or low-income housing communities.

These properties were often viewed as not lucrative or appealing in comparison to traditional commercial or high-end residential assets.

However, Zell understood a basic fact: the need for inexpensive housing would keep increasing, and manufactured housing presented consistent revenue streams because of its lower turnover rates and the expensive process of moving homes.

By entering this industry, Zell showed that he was not discouraged by the stigma or the presumptions of his fellow investors.

His investments in manufactured housing quickly became a highly profitable part of his portfolio, consistently generating returns even in times of economic decline.

Zell not only accepted the instability of a quiet market but also recognized the hidden need, investing in a long-lasting movement that went unnoticed by other investors.

This method was applied to Zell's global enterprises as well. During the 1990s, he started putting money into developing markets such as Latin America and Eastern Europe.

During that period, these markets were seen as questionable because of political uncertainty, inadequate legal structures, and unstable currencies.

However, Zell looked past the dangers. He acknowledged that these economies were going through fast urbanization and had increasing needs for commercial and residential properties.

Zell established himself as a trailblazer by entering these markets early and frequently collaborating with local developers to minimize risk and gain important local knowledge. Zell's ability to form strategic partnerships helped him manage the uncertainties of investing in emerging markets.

By partnering with experts in the region and utilizing their expertise, he reduced the risks linked to these investments.

His strategy in high-stakes, global markets showed that he wasn't impulsively chasing opportunities; instead, he was carefully preparing for both the dangers and benefits, believing in his capacity to adjust and react to unexpected shifts.

Zell's beliefs on risk were also applied to his opinions on diversification. While many investors spread out their investments across different types of assets to minimize risk, Zell concentrated on spreading out his investments within the real estate industry.

Instead of straying too far from his area of expertise, Zell sought variety in the types of properties he purchased, including office buildings, student housing, and mobile home parks.

This method enabled him to create a durable portfolio that could withstand economic downturns, as various property types reacted differently to market changes.

One of Zell's riskiest decisions was venturing into the newspaper sector by purchasing the Tribune Company in 2007.

During that period, the newspaper sector was experiencing significant upheaval because of the emergence of digital media, with numerous individuals seeing it as a declining industry.

Yet Zell recognized promise while others perceived destruction. He was confident that by implementing new management techniques and changing the company's strategy, he could revitalize the business.

Despite the Tribune acquisition being one of Zell's less successful endeavors, his readiness to enter a risky industry highlighted his commitment to making daring decisions, even in uncertain circumstances.

For Zell, instead of fearing risk, he viewed it as an essential part of every opportunity.

His well-thought-out choices in risky markets were not spur-of-the-moment risks but rather came from thorough analysis, strategic partnerships, and knowledge of enduring patterns.

His success was based on embracing uncertainty and looking for alternative investments.

3.2 Timing the Market: How Zell Mastered the Cycles of Real Estate

In addition to accepting risk, Zell showed a special talent for timing his investments accurately, capitalizing on market cycles to increase profits. Real estate goes through natural cycles, shifting between periods of fast expansion and declines with adjustments.

Zell was successful in maneuvering through these cycles because he believed that each boom was fleeting, and each bust presented a chance for growth.

Zell's strategy for market timing was based on waiting patiently. He was ready to endure periods of decline when prices would decrease and properties could be purchased for less money.

This viewpoint enabled him to obtain important assets in downturns, confident that the economic situation would get better over time. His patience and contrarian mindset led him to act differently from other investors by purchasing properties at significantly lower prices during downturns.

One of the most remarkable instances of Zell's market timing was his involvement in the commercial real estate boom of the 1990s.

Following the savings and loan crisis in the late 1980s, the real estate market experienced a sharp decline, resulting in record-low property values nationwide.

Numerous investors viewed commercial real estate as a hazardous asset category. Zell, on the other hand, viewed this as a chance to make a purchase.

He started purchasing struggling office buildings and commercial properties, convinced that the market would recover. As a result, Zell's assets saw a significant increase in worth, generating large profits and confirming his reputation as an expert in timing the market.

Zell demonstrated good timing in his sales strategy as well. In the same way, he was strict about entering markets in times of decline, he was just as strict about leaving them in times of high.

In 2007, Zell arranged the $39 billion sale of Equity Office Properties Trust (EOP), the biggest office building owner in the United States, to Blackstone Group.

Zell made this sale when the market was booming, right before the 2008 financial crisis caused a sharp drop in real estate prices. Selling at the market peak allowed Zell to prevent the significant losses that would have occurred if he had kept the portfolio during the recession.

This sale demonstrated Zell's knowledge of real estate market fluctuations. He was aware that the market was too hot, with property prices climbing to unsustainable heights, so he seized the chance to sell at the highest value.

Zell's choice to offload EOP not only protected his profits but also emphasized his commitment to staying ready for the upcoming cycle.

Timing the market for Zell meant identifying when assets were too expensive and having the self-control to sell, even in a bullish market. Zell's impeccable timing not only applied to specific properties and portfolios but also to his strategic decisions in up-and-coming industries.

His ability to predict changes in consumer needs was shown when he chose to invest in student housing and manufactured housing in times of low demand.

Zell understood that with the increase in housing prices, there would be a higher demand for affordable housing options, making student and manufactured housing appealing long-term investments.

Zell gained an advantage over competitors by getting into these industries early and benefited as they expanded.

Besides his grasp of cycles, Zell also highlighted the significance of being adaptable.

Various factors, such as economic policies and global events, impact real estate markets, and Zell understood that inflexible strategies could be harmful.

His ability to adapt enabled him to make changes as needed, whether it involved entering a fresh market, liquidating assets, or investigating various types of property.

Zell's ability to adapt was crucial for his success in market timing, as it allowed him to swiftly react to shifting conditions and steer clear of slowdowns.

In the end, Zell's expertise in market cycles was developed through patience, a contrarian mindset, and flexibility.

He was patient for the perfect timing, sometimes entering when others were leaving, and was just as ready to sell at the peak, unaffected by the temptation of further profits.

Zell's market timing did not involve accurately forecasting the future, but rather comprehending cycles and being ready to take action when conditions matched his principles.

Conclusion

Sam Zell achieved success in the real estate industry due to his deliberate handling of risk and his grasp on market timing.

He welcomed uncertainty, seeing opportunity in high-stakes markets others viewed as risky, and he excelled at timing the market, purchasing during lows and selling during highs.

Zell's skill in maneuvering through real estate market fluctuations allowed him to construct a strong, lucrative business domain, establishing himself as a prominent figure in the industry.

CHAPTER 4

BUILDING AN EMPIRE

4.1 From Office Spaces to Trailer Parks: Diversifying the Portfolio

Sam Zell achieved success by being open to unconventional assets and spreading his real estate investments across various sectors.

He found worth in real estate that was often overlooked or underestimated, ranging from commercial buildings in thriving cities to mobile home parks serving the affordable housing sector.

This method of diversification aimed not only to broaden his scope but also to create a strong portfolio that could endure market changes by investing in various asset classes with distinct risk and reward characteristics.

Zell began with office spaces, an industry he was familiar with and considered a dependable source of income.

His first experience in office real estate helped him learn the fundamentals of overseeing large properties and comprehending tenant requirements.

Zell discovered the importance of targeting underappreciated office buildings, acquiring them at a lower cost, enhancing them with renovations and better administration, and ultimately earning a steady income from leasing agreements.

This initial achievement formed the basis of Zell's investing strategy: identify underpriced assets, enhance their value, and establish a consistent source of income.

Still, Zell understood that depending only on office spaces would restrict his potential to grow and expose his portfolio to fluctuations in the market.

The real estate market has natural cycles, and demand for office space can vary significantly based on economic factors.

This discovery prompted him to look for chances beyond conventional office buildings, delving into areas such as student housing, industrial spaces, and trailer parks. Different types of property catered to distinct market segments, each carrying different levels of risk, competition, and potential for cash flow.

Zell made a bold and unexpected move by entering the manufactured housing sector, which initially caused surprise within the industry.

Manufactured housing, also known as mobile home parks, was frequently seen as a low-end investment, considered unattractive, and faced with management difficulties.

However, Zell noticed something that others overlooked: reliable renters who were less inclined to relocate, consistent income streams, and a type of investment that was unaffected by numerous issues affecting conventional property markets. His business, Equity LifeStyle Properties (ELS), emerged as one of the biggest proprietors of manufactured home communities nationwide.

This courageous decision expanded his investments and solidified Zell's reputation as an innovator capable of identifying potential in situations deemed risky by others.

Zell also focused on student housing as another sector. The need for student housing remained steady and expected, fueled by the continuous arrival of college students annually.

Zell understood that student housing has a constant rotation of tenants and a built-in market, unlike office spaces or commercial buildings. His decision to invest in student housing demonstrated his skill in accessing secure, income-producing assets and expanding his portfolio diversification.

Student housing was changed by Zell to become a profitable part of his portfolio, bringing in consistent income and strengthening the overall stability of his investments.

Zell's readiness to accept diversification also expanded to encompass geographic diversity. He understood that real estate markets in diverse areas did not always change together, so by investing in different places—both within the United

States and internationally—he could better protect his portfolio from economic downturns.

For instance, as certain areas were decreasing, others were expanding, enabling him to manage risks and take advantage of opportunities in all regions.

His investments covered office spaces in busy cities, affordable housing in suburbs, and manufactured housing in rural areas, all catering to different demographics and needs.

Zell's interest in diversification also drove him to investigate global real estate markets. In the 1990s, he explored opportunities in Latin America and Eastern Europe, realizing potential in new markets driven by urbanization and economic expansion, leading to an increased need for housing and commercial properties.

By expanding his investments globally, Zell took advantage of fast-growing areas and diversified his investments into markets with varying economic cycles from the U.S.

This decision strengthened his reputation as a daring investor who was willing to explore new territories for potential rewards.

Diversification was not just a random pursuit for Zell, but a deliberate tactic to build a well-rounded portfolio able to withstand economic downturns.

His readiness to accept non-traditional assets, including various property types and locations, set the foundation for the strong and flexible empire that would shape his legacy.

His varied strategy enabled him to survive economic downturns, take advantage of economic upturns, and outpace rivals, establishing him as a highly adaptable and impactful presence in the real estate sector.

4.2 The Importance of Personnel: Building a Successful Team

Despite Zell's success being attributed to his impressive investment skills and willingness to take risks, he was also recognized for his dedication to forming a united and powerful team.

Zell realized that he couldn't create an empire on his own; having the correct individuals on board was crucial for carrying out his vision, handling intricate projects, and overcoming the obstacles of entering new markets.

His focus on discovering and fostering talent became a fundamental aspect of his approach, allowing him to expand his business while upholding a strong level of operational performance.

Zell's method of building teams was unconventional, demonstrating his distinct leadership style and focus on working together. He sought individuals who were also ready to question the current situation and approach real estate with fresh perspectives.

He looked for people who were entrepreneurial, resilient, and willing to challenge traditional thinking.

According to Zell, the perfect team member was someone who not only had skills but also had a passion for risk and innovation.

He desired team members who could offer new viewpoints, spot missed chances, and assist him in realizing his long-term goals.

One of the main principles Zell used when putting together his team was giving people the ability to take control of their projects. He motivated his team to behave as entrepreneurs within the company, granting them the freedom to make choices and the responsibility to follow through.

This method promoted a mindset of accountability and proactivity, inspiring team members to exceed expectations in order to achieve outcomes.

Zell's focus on empowering employees led to a vibrant workplace that drew in ambitious individuals looking to leave their impact.

Zell also realized the significance of cultivating commitment among his team members. He thought that loyalty went both ways: if he stayed loyal to his team and gave them chances to grow, they would also be loyal to him in return. This belief prompted him to establish a work environment that prioritized honesty, confidence, and straightforward dialogue.

Zell had a reputation for being straightforward and honest with his team, anticipating the same in response.

Through promoting honesty and loyalty, Zell established a team that was both highly skilled and fully dedicated to the company's success and projects.

Bob Lurie, a partner and close friend, was one of Zell's most reliable lieutenants who played a crucial part in Zell's venture.

Lurie supported Zell's vision and assisted him in carrying out numerous deals that shaped the company's path. The relationship between Zell and Lurie was formed based on mutual admiration, confidence, and a common desire for creativity.

As a team, they became a strong duo that propelled the company's expansion with daring investments and thoughtful acquisitions.

Zell learned from Lurie's example that having the right people in key positions is crucial, and he applied this lesson as he grew his empire.

Zell also developed a group of experienced managers and specialists besides Lurie, who were able to oversee various aspects of the business such as property management, financing, and legal issues. He understood that constructing an empire needed specific expertise and abilities, therefore he surrounded himself with experts who could contribute their skills in various fields.

Zell appreciated team members who were skilled in their fields and shared his vision and beliefs.

The combination of skills and cultural compatibility made sure the team could collaborate effectively, adjusting to fresh obstacles as the business expanded.

Zell also prioritized training and development. He put resources into the development of his team, providing chances for education and progress within the company. By developing skills from within, Zell created a team that was not just highly skilled but also very loyal to the company.

This method aided him in keeping high-quality employees, decreasing turnover, and maintaining consistency in overseeing intricate projects.

Zell's dedication to his team's development solidified his image as a leader who prioritized people over profits.

In the end, Zell's dedication to forming a powerful, skilled team played a crucial role in his achievements.

His focus on commitment, giving power, and matching cultures resulted in a workplace that drew in highly skilled individuals and enabled them to succeed. The team he put together became the foundation of his empire, fueling the company's expansion and guaranteeing its strength amidst obstacles.

Zell's method of building teams focused on establishing a culture of excellence, creativity, and mutual respect, rather than just filling roles, to drive his vision forward.

Conclusion

Sam Zell's success stems from his investment tactics, dedication to diversification, and the quality of his team. By incorporating various types of assets and locations, he built a strong portfolio able to handle changes in the economy. Simultaneously, he was able to carry out his vision with precision and consistency by focusing on building a skilled and dedicated team.

CHAPTER 5

BREAKING CONVENTIONS

5.1 The Contrarian Mindset: Zell's Approach to Conventional Wisdom

Since the beginning of his professional journey, Sam Zell has turned away from conventional methods and adopted a mindset that goes against the norm, a belief that influenced a lot of his prosperous projects.

Being a contrarian for Zell wasn't just rebelling for the sake of it; it was a tactical decision based on a clear understanding of where others saw boundaries or overlooked possibilities.

His method turned possible dangers into chances, showcasing how defying norms can result in massive accomplishments in his career.

Zell's strategy in the real estate sector focused on challenging the current norms.

During the 1970s, the real estate industry was commonly viewed as stable and reliable, mainly centered around familiar markets and conventional property categories.

Zell thought that the real estate sector, just like other industries, could experience cycles, underestimate assets, and offer niche chances.

While some saw expected profit margins, Zell recognized undervalued assets that had the potential for higher returns with proper management. Zell's unconventional approach was defined by his readiness to adopt unusual asset classes and geographic locations.

During the early 1970s, Zell ventured into troubled assets, mainly office buildings, a move seen as daring at that time.

Instead of buying new properties in well-established areas, he looked for buildings that were deteriorating and required investment, innovative leasing strategies, or just a different approach to management.

His emphasis on troubled assets showed that he believed that successful investing often involved looking into places that others were too wary to explore. Zell's contrarian approach also included his fascination with manufactured housing, specifically trailer parks, which were often considered unappealing and "lowbrow" by many investors.

Zell realized that the lower-income demographics served by manufactured housing provided a consistent, typically recession-resistant source of income.

When he bought these properties, he recognized that he was investing in a market with high demand and low competition, allowing him to establish a leading position.

This approach not only broadened his portfolio but also highlighted Zell's belief in the importance of exploring untapped areas where other investors were reluctant to venture.

Zell's way of thinking was also defined by consistently questioning commonly held beliefs, especially ones that influenced market trends.

Frequently, he cited the tendency of investors to follow the crowd as a key reason for financial bubbles, inflated valuations, and misguided investment decisions.

Zell was doubtful of market trends that were widely trusted, such as the commonly accepted "bigger is better" philosophy in real estate. Instead of chasing after fancy skyscrapers and top-notch commercial properties in big cities like others did, Zell concentrated on ignored markets and types of assets.

This strategy enabled him to take advantage of opportunities that were insulated from the uncertainties of regular competition.

During the late 1980s, Zell demonstrated his contrarian viewpoint when commercial real estate markets experienced excessive overbuilding.

This excess of office space, caused by extensive development over the years, was bound to be corrected, and Zell predicted it earlier than others.

He started to sell office buildings, understanding that an oversupply and declining demand would cause prices to decrease sooner or later. His choice to sell off assets before the crash enabled him to steer clear of the losses faced by his rivals and left him with funds available for investment once prices hit rock bottom.

This forward-thinking decision showcased Zell's skill in thinking long-term rather than focusing on immediate profits, preparing himself for future success by going against the market trend.

Zell's contrarian approach wasn't just about the assets he pursued, but also about how he ran his businesses.

Contrary to other real estate magnates who favored strict control and hierarchical structures, Zell promoted a flexible and open corporate environment that emphasized innovation and accountability.

He established a setting in which staff members were encouraged to challenge assumptions and suggest innovative ideas, convinced that a variety of viewpoints would help his companies stay flexible and responsive.

This receptiveness to fresh concepts was another aspect of his unique method, enabling him to utilize his team's knowledge while steering clear of the dangers of stagnation.

Zell believed that achieving success in real estate primarily involved perception - recognizing value instead of risk and seeing potential instead of failure where others did not. This method necessitated more than just a strong comprehension of market patterns; it also required a readiness to accept unpredictability and have faith in his gut feelings.

Zell's unconventional way of thinking laid the groundwork for his approach, allowing him to succeed in various economic conditions and distinguish himself from other real estate investors.

5.2 Converting Problems into Possibilities: Managing Economic Declines

Financial downturns can be particularly troublesome for investors, especially in the real estate sector, as they can greatly affect asset values and cash flows during recessions. For the majority, these stages are characterized by cutting back, reducing costs, and a cautious strategy to protect capital.

Yet, Zell viewed economic downturns as a favorable environment for expansion, times when there were plenty of opportunities for those who were ready to take strategic risks.

His success was attributed as much to his resilience in tough times as it was to his ability to make profits during periods of growth.

One of the most severe economic downturns Zell dealt with was the Savings and Loan Crisis in the late 1980s and early 1990s. In this time frame, many savings and loan institutions in the United States experienced financial trouble because of risky lending practices and heavily leveraged investments in real estate.

With the failure of these institutions, numerous distressed properties flooded the market and were eventually sold by the government for a fraction of their initial price.

Although many investors avoided these properties due to the potential for more losses, Zell viewed them as a unique chance to purchase. He promptly utilized his resources to purchase undervalued assets at low prices, anticipating the market would bounce back. Zell's ability to stay composed and make quick decisions during the Savings and Loan Crisis showcased his success.

This event made him more confident in the idea that crises are usually optimal for investing, as they cause assets to be undervalued due to market panic.

Through buying these troubled properties and keeping them until the market improved, Zell accumulated substantial wealth while his rivals were recovering from their losses.

His actions in the crisis highlighted his dedication to seeing difficulties as chances rather than risks.

Zell's response to economic downturns was also marked by a disciplined, opportunistic view of debt.

During times of economic growth, numerous property investors used high levels of borrowing, but Zell opted for a cautious approach to debt, refraining from excessive leveraging despite low interest rates.

This strategy allowed him the freedom to take advantage of opportunities when the market was down, as he wasn't burdened by financial commitments that restricted his ability to make moves.

Zell frequently took advantage of downturns to purchase troubled assets from companies with too much debt, using his cash reserves and good credit to buy assets on favorable terms. Zell made a notable move during the peak of the U.S. real estate bubble in 2007.

Feeling that the market was too hot and ready for a downturn, Zell arranged one of the biggest real estate deals ever by selling his office-building empire, Equity Office Properties Trust, to the Blackstone Group for $39 billion.

The timing was perfect; in less than a year, the worldwide economic crisis struck, destroying property values and putting many investors in a difficult situation.

Zell's choice to sell at the peak of the market enabled him to avoid the financial downturn that affected the industry, solidifying his reputation as a skilled market timer and risk manager. Zell's skill in taking advantage of economic downturns was not restricted to only the local markets; he also implemented this approach on a global scale.

During the 1990s, he broadened his presence to Latin America and Eastern Europe, areas facing economic difficulties but with promising growth opportunities.

Through investing in struggling assets and businesses in developing markets, Zell established a presence in economies that would eventually see significant growth.

His eagerness to engage in these markets during difficult times showcased his confidence in the enduring benefits of contrarian investing, along with his grasp of the cyclical patterns of economic development.

Along with his strategic purchases, Zell also focused on operational effectiveness during periods of economic decline.

He thought that difficult times were a chance to make operations more efficient, cut expenses, and enhance cash flow, enabling his businesses to come out of downturns even more robust.

This methodical way of managing costs allowed Zell to endure economic challenges without compromising the financial stability of his businesses.

He saw downturns as an opportunity to assess the strength of his portfolio and pinpoint areas for enhancement, creating a culture of flexibility that defined his achievements.

Zell's unconventional strategy during economic downturns, viewing them as chances for growth instead of hindrances, was a key element of his professional success.

By staying disciplined, patient, and prepared to take action while others hesitated, he transformed obstacles into opportunities for advancement.

His skill in maneuvering through economic downturns not only protected his riches but also solidified his reputation as a forward-thinking investor who could succeed in any market condition.

Conclusion

Sam Zell's professional journey was influenced by his tendency to think differently and his steadfast conviction that obstacles could be turned into advantages.

Zell's ability to defy norms in his approach to asset classes, question market trends, and invest during downturns enabled him to create a long-lasting empire.

CHAPTER 6

THE ZELL WAY: PRINCIPLES FOR SUCCESS

6.1 Resilience and Grit: Overcoming Setbacks in Business and Life

During his professional journey, Sam Zell established himself as a skilled real estate investor and a determined entrepreneur who was able to conquer numerous challenges due to his perseverance.

Zell's path was anything but straightforward, featuring periods of money troubles, economic downturns, and personal challenges that put his determination to the test.

However, these incidents only strengthened his conviction in the importance of resilience for achieving success, enabling him to turn obstacles into chances.

From a young age, Zell displayed indicators of the determination that would ultimately characterize his professional path.

He was brought up in Chicago by Polish immigrant parents who fled the Holocaust, instilling in him values of hard work, resourcefulness, and resilience in the face of challenges.

His parents taught him to have a strong appreciation for persistence and to understand that, even though life is unpredictable, one can overcome obstacles with determination and resilience.

Having been exposed to resilience at an early age, shaped his outlook as he entered the fields of real estate and business, equipping him with the mental strength to confront challenges directly.

One of the first hurdles Zell encountered in his professional journey was in the 1970s when he entered the troubled properties sector, which was considered risky and avoided by many investors.

He did not have enough money saved up or a solid reputation to back up his investments at that point. While buying and overseeing troubled assets, he faced considerable financial dangers, ranging from structures needing extensive renovations to renters failing to pay rent.

Zell learned from his early experiences managing these properties the significance of toughness in enduring financial instability and the patience required to attain profitable results.

Rather than quitting, he increased his efforts and worked nonstop to transform underperforming properties into lucrative investments.

During this time, Zell learned that setbacks weren't failures but chances to improve, adjust, and become more resilient.

Zell faced even more challenges in the late 1980s during the Savings and Loan Crisis, a time characterized by extensive financial upheaval and a rise in troubled real estate assets.

The crisis had the potential to be a big hurdle for Zell, but he viewed it as a chance for growth.

Through persistence and determination, he used his resources effectively to purchase properties for a fraction of their actual worth.

His belief in resilience as a key to success was showcased when he successfully navigated the crisis and emerged even stronger.

He demonstrated that seeing setbacks as temporary challenges, not impossible hurdles, was crucial for achieving long-term success, especially in difficult situations.

Zell believed that resilience involved more than just handling financial difficulties; it also meant remaining committed to one's goals despite outside influences.

During his professional journey, he faced critics who doubted his unconventional investment decisions and contrary strategy.

His emphasis on undervalued and distressed assets was met with skepticism by numerous individuals in the real estate sector, who considered his tactics to be excessively hazardous. Still, Zell stayed firm, relying on his gut feelings and refusing to just go along with the crowd.

His ability to remain determined in the face of negative feedback enabled him to maintain his dedication to his innovative strategy, ultimately resulting in impressive accomplishments.

Zell's dedication to resilience was also evident in his personal life. Aside from his career difficulties, he also experienced personal tragedies and medical problems, all of which necessitated him to rely on his inner resilience.

He freely admitted that resilience was not a skill acquired quickly, but instead required years of confronting and conquering obstacles to develop. Zell demonstrated the strength of resilience in both business and life by facing challenges with optimism and determination toward his objectives.

Resilience in Zell's case was both a strategic approach and a mentality. He saw challenges as chances to grow, adjusting his strategies and enhancing his techniques with every obstacle encountered.

His skill in adapting and never giving up enabled him to transform setbacks into stepping stones for future achievements, solidifying his image as a determined entrepreneur.

Zell believed that the key to success lay in facing challenges with courage and conviction, rather than avoiding them. This emphasis on resilience was his guiding principle.

6.2 The Long Game: Zell's Enduring Philosophy on Wealth and Legacy

As Sam Zell advanced in his career and accumulated wealth, his perspective on success changed to include not just financial accomplishments but also the larger influence he aimed to have.

Zell's attitude towards wealth was always focused on long-term success and lasting recognition. Instead, he chose to focus on sustainable growth, strategic investments, and creating a long-lasting legacy by taking a long-term perspective.

His dedication to focusing on the "long game" became a key feature of his professional journey, influencing his choices and molding his perspective on what lies ahead.

Since the start, Zell based his real estate strategy on patience and a thorough knowledge of market fluctuations.

Early on, he realized that real estate, just like many other investments, could experience fluctuations, emphasizing the importance of timing.

Instead of hastily entering into agreements for quick profits, he preferred to be patient and wait for the appropriate chances to come along. Having a long-term outlook enabled him to make strategic decisions, steering clear of the risky thinking that frequently misled his peers.

Zell's ability to patiently accumulate wealth was crucial, as he concentrated on developing a collection of assets with lasting value instead of seeking immediate profits.

One of Zell's most well-known moves was when he sold Equity Office Properties Trust in 2007 as part of his long-term strategy.

Feeling that the commercial real estate market was reaching its highest point, Zell arranged the sale of his office-building business to Blackstone Group for $39 billion, just before the onset of the global financial crisis. He managed to make a significant profit by selling when the market was high, avoiding the significant losses that occurred after the crash.

This decision showcased Zell's skill in timing his choices based on long-term goals, placing himself for continued success as others faced challenges in bouncing back.

Zell believed in building relationships and creating a culture of trust within his organizations as part of playing the long game.

He thought that riches were not solely determined by money but also by the relationships one developed on their journey. Zell assembled a team of skilled individuals, several of whom turned into enduring partners and collaborators.

His dedication to establishing solid relationships enabled him to form a reliable team of advisors and talented individuals who supported the expansion of his businesses.

Zell believed that success depended on building strong relationships, highlighting the importance of teamwork, loyalty, and mutual respect in creating lasting change.

Aside from his business ventures, Zell's views on wealth and legacy were influenced by his dedication to charitable giving. As his wealth increased, he felt obliged to give back to society by using his resources. Zell's charitable activities covered a wide range of areas, including education, healthcare, and the arts.

He thought that riches should be utilized to create a beneficial impact on society, backing causes that reflected his beliefs and encouraging chances for others.

His acts of charity showed his wish to create a lasting impact, not only benefiting himself but also ensuring a better tomorrow for the next generations.

Zell's support for educational institutions was one of his most notable philanthropic endeavors.

He generously gave a large sum of money to the University of Michigan, his former school, to create the Zell Lurie Institute for

Entrepreneurial Studies. His goal with this program was to motivate and provide the necessary tools and resources for the upcoming entrepreneurs to be successful.

Zell believed in the importance of education because he thought that knowledge and opportunity were crucial for success and that by supporting education, he could have a positive impact on society.

Zell's views on riches and heritage were clear in the way he handled succession planning as well.

Acknowledging that his businesses were a reflection of his vision, he made sure they would prosper even after he left. He thought that creating a solid legacy involved thoughtful preparation, so he made sure to proactively ready his businesses for what lay ahead.

Zell's dedication to succession planning showed his recognition of the significance of continuity, along with his wish to establish organizations that would maintain his principles and carry on his tradition of innovation and excellence.

Ultimately, Zell believed that success in the long game should not solely focus on financial gain. To him, riches were a resource to gain independence, bring about change, and leave a permanent impression.

His lasting beliefs about wealth and legacy stressed the significance of creating something that could withstand time, motivating others to look beyond instant outcomes and concentrate on the broader view. Zell's dedication to the long-term strategy influenced his career decisions and enabled him to succeed on his terms.

Conclusion

Sam Zell's strategy for success was characterized by his principles of resilience, patience, and a focus on the long term.

Through perseverance in the face of challenges, keeping a focus on the future, and creating a lasting impact, Zell established a career that went beyond traditional notions of wealth.

His perspective on resilience and legacy provides valuable lessons for those hoping to become entrepreneurs and investors, emphasizing the significance of looking toward the future and concentrating on creating enduring impacts.

CHAPTER 7

THE REAL ESTATE RENEGADE'S LEGACY

7.1 Philanthropy and Impact: Zell's Influence Beyond Real Estate

Sam Zell's impact goes beyond his impressive success in the real estate industry; it includes a deep dedication to charitable giving and a goal to make a lasting difference in society.

While constructing his billion-dollar empire, Zell was always mindful of the duties that came with his riches.

He adopted the idea that genuine success is determined not only by making money but also by the ability to positively impact the world. Through a variety of charitable projects, Zell has aimed to improve communities, support education, and encourage innovation, making a lasting impact that mirrors his beliefs and goals.

Zell's charitable path is based on his conviction that education is a key catalyst for transformation. He acknowledged that quality education gives individuals opportunities and helps them reach their full potential.

This knowledge prompted him to make substantial investments in educational establishments, especially at the University of Michigan, where he had previously attended.

His dedication to fostering future entrepreneurs is demonstrated through his establishment of the Zell Lurie Institute for Entrepreneurial Studies at the university.

The main goal of the Zell Lurie Institute is to give students hands-on experience and guidance in entrepreneurship, equipping them with the necessary tools and resources for success in the business world.

Zell realized that entrepreneurship extends beyond just launching companies; it involves finding answers to issues and stimulating economic development.

His goal was to instill the values of resilience and innovation in aspiring entrepreneurs by providing them with educational support, reflecting the principles that had guided him in his career.

In addition to higher education, Zell has supported efforts to advance social justice and improve communities.

He has supported organizations that help disadvantaged communities, with a focus on housing, healthcare, and economic empowerment.

Zell has sought to combat systemic inequalities by giving resources and opportunities to those who may be marginalized.

His entrepreneurial nature is in harmony with his faith in the strength of community, as he aims to establish spaces that foster individual growth and achievement. Zell's philanthropic legacy also leaves a mark on the arts and culture world.

He has consistently backed multiple cultural establishments, acknowledging the significance of the arts in enhancing society.

Zell's support for museums, theaters, and other artistic projects has nurtured creativity and the appreciation of the arts.

His backing of projects that encourage cultural awareness showcases his faith in the ability of creativity to spark change and unite individuals.

Zell has not only provided financial support but has also been engaged in mentoring and leading philanthropic initiatives.

He has interacted with young entrepreneurs and aspiring business leaders, offering his experiences and insights to assist them in navigating the intricacies of the business world.

Zell has motivated numerous people to follow their interests and achieve their goals through talks, workshops, and one-on-one guidance.

His openness in sharing his experiences and insights motivates future innovators and disruptors. Zell's charitable impact is defined by a dedication to creativity and flexibility. He understands that social issues are always changing and finding solutions for them involves thinking outside the box.

Consequently, he has backed projects that utilize technology and innovation to promote positive transformations.

By putting his money into organizations that prioritize innovative strategies, Zell has established himself as a driver of change, showing that philanthropy can effectively drive societal change.

Zell's philanthropic influence can be seen in the individuals he has helped and the organizations he has backed. His impact is not just related to donating money, but also to promoting a mindset of reciprocity.

Zell's conviction that all individuals have a part to contribute to improving the world is evident in his philanthropic pursuits.

He urges others to participate in his mission, stressing that real success is determined by the positive impact one can make in their community.

Zell's impact goes beyond just his charitable work; it motivates a wider group of entrepreneurs and business executives.

His dedication to using his wealth for social causes has inspired other members of the business community to participate in philanthropy, creating a spirit of giving that goes beyond personal achievement.

Zell sets an example for successful entrepreneurs by promoting corporate social responsibility and demonstrating how resources can be used to make a significant impact.

Ultimately, Sam Zell's charitable activities mirror his beliefs, perspective, and dedication to creating a positive impact on the world.

His impact extends further than just real estate, as he aims to uplift communities, empower individuals, and motivate the future generation of entrepreneurs.

By promoting education, involving the community, and backing the arts, Zell has established a lasting impact reflecting resilience, innovation, and social responsibility.

7.2 Zell's Blueprint for Future Entrepreneurs: Lessons for the Next Generation

Sam Zell, a self-made billionaire and prominent figure in real estate, has earned great respect for his business skills and unconventional entrepreneurship.

During his professional journey, he has faced obstacles, made use of chances, and created a plan for achieving success that hopeful business people can take notes from.

By condensing his experiences into practical lessons, Zell offers invaluable guidance for individuals looking to navigate their way in the business world. Zell teaches a fundamental lesson about the significance of adopting a contrarian mindset.

During his career, he has continuously pushed back against traditional beliefs and explored markets and opportunities that were considered too risky or unattractive by others.

Zell attributes his success to his ability to think independently and challenge the established norms.

He motivates aspiring entrepreneurs to develop their perspectives, understanding that genuine innovation frequently comes from questioning current standards.

Zell's unconventional way of thinking is apparent in his investment approach, specifically his concentration on discounted and troubled assets.

Even though many investors were hesitant to invest in those properties, Zell saw the opportunity for high returns by putting money into what others ignored.

He educates hopeful entrepreneurs on how opportunities can be found in unforeseen places, and by being open to taking strategic risks, they can discover value that others overlook.

Another crucial takeaway from Zell's strategy is the significance of being resilient and adaptable. Despite encountering multiple setbacks and economic downturns, he has continued to grow stronger throughout his career.

Zell stresses that encountering failure is a necessary aspect of the entrepreneurial path and that being able to adjust and grow from obstacles is crucial for sustained success.

Entrepreneurs who are looking to start their own business are advised to see failure as a chance to learn and grow, using it as a stepping stone to achieve success in the future.

Zell also promotes the significance of keeping a long-term outlook, in addition to resilience. He understands that it takes time and commitment to build a successful business and that short-term outcomes should not distract from the long-term goal. Zell motivates future business owners to establish distinct objectives and stay concentrated on their goals, acknowledging that real achievement takes time and dedication, not just quick results.

Entrepreneurs can achieve lasting impact and build sustainable businesses by making sustainable growth a priority and encouraging a culture of innovation.

Zell also highlights the importance of connections and building relationships in the business industry.

During his professional journey, he has developed close relationships with other business owners, investors, and key figures in the industry, understanding the importance of working together and exchanging ideas.

He urges upcoming entrepreneurs to develop connections that promote shared assistance, guidance, and working together.

Entrepreneurs can enhance their growth by surrounding themselves with similar individuals, allowing them to access valuable resources and gain insights.

Moreover, Zell emphasizes the significance of understanding financial concepts and making strategic choices.

He thinks that potential entrepreneurs should gain a profound comprehension of their financial situation, focusing on budgeting, managing cash flow, and investment tactics. Entrepreneurs can move their businesses forward by making informed decisions through gaining financial knowledge.

Zell's focus on financial literacy demonstrates his opinion that achieving success in entrepreneurship requires more than just a good idea - it also involves effective execution.

Zell's experiences also show the importance of being able to adapt in the face of change.

The business environment is always changing, impacted by technological progress, changing consumer choices, and economic variability. Zell advises aspiring entrepreneurs to stay updated and be prepared to adjust their strategies when needed.

Entrepreneurs can stay competitive and set themselves up for success in a fast-paced market by embracing change and taking advantage of new opportunities.

Additionally, Zell's dedication to charitable giving provides a strong example for entrepreneurs in training.

He stresses that real success involves benefiting society and using one's resources for the common good.

Entrepreneurs can establish a lasting impact by contributing to charitable initiatives and backing causes that hold personal significance to them, going beyond their professional achievements. Zell motivates aspiring entrepreneurs to think about their duty to give back and create a positive impact in their communities, promoting a social responsibility culture.

To sum up, Sam Zell's guidelines for hopeful entrepreneurs are based on a contrary mindset, endurance, future-oriented outlook, solid connections, financial knowledge, flexibility, and dedication to charitable efforts.

His experiences and insights offer valuable advice for individuals looking to navigate the complexities of entrepreneurship.

By adopting these beliefs, young entrepreneurs can pave their way to success by establishing businesses that mirror their principles and have a positive influence on society.

Conclusion

Sam Zell's reputation as a real estate trailblazer and generous donor showcases the importance of determination, creativity, and dedication to charity.

His charitable efforts and advice for hopeful business owners act as a beacon for upcoming generations, motivating them to chase their aspirations and create a beneficial influence on society.

www.ingramcontent.com/pod-product-compliance
Lightning Source LLC
Chambersburg PA
CBHW071514220526
45472CB00003B/1025